The Ultimate Guide to iOS 17.0.1 Features

Get the Most Out of Your iPhone

George Anvil

Table of contents

Chapter 7: Conclusion

Chapter 1: Introduction

1.1 What is this chapter about?

Welcome to the beginning of your journey into the world of iOS 17.0.1 and the boundless capabilities of your iPhone. In this chapter, we'll set the stage for the adventure that lies ahead. Let's break it down:

Imagine for a moment that your iPhone is not just a phone. It's a powerhouse of technology, a digital Swiss Army knife that can do so much more than make calls. It's your connection to the world, your personal assistant, your entertainment hub, and your productivity tool, all rolled into one sleek device.

But here's the catch – with all this incredible power comes complexity. iPhones are loaded with features, apps, and settings that can be daunting to navigate, especially when a new iOS update like 17.0.1 rolls in.

You might be wondering, "How do I make the most of it all? How do I ensure that my iPhone is not just a gadget, but a true companion in my daily life?"

Well, that's precisely what this guide is all about – helping you unlock the full potential of your iPhone, particularly in the context of iOS 17.0.1. We're here to make the complex simple, to turn the daunting into doable, and to ensure that you can confidently use your iPhone for everything it's designed for.

1.2 Why is it important to get the most out of your iPhone?

Your iPhone is more than just a piece of technology; it's a gateway to a world of possibilities. Let's unpack why it's crucial to harness its full potential:

1. Versatility: Your iPhone is a versatile tool, capable of serving multiple roles in your life. It's your communication hub, your task manager, your entertainment source, and even your creativity canvas. To fully benefit from this versatility, you need to explore and understand its many features.

2. Efficiency: In today's fast-paced world, time is precious. Your iPhone can streamline tasks, from managing your schedule to helping you find information instantly. The more you know about its capabilities, the more efficiently you can navigate your daily life.

3. Connection: Staying connected is vital. Whether it's keeping in touch with loved ones, collaborating with colleagues, or engaging with your community, your iPhone is your digital bridge. Learning how to use its features enhances your ability to connect effectively.

4. Productivity: Your iPhone can be a powerful productivity tool. It can help you work on the go, manage projects, and access important documents. Knowing its features can significantly boost your productivity.

5. Innovation: iOS updates like 17.0.1 bring new features and improvements, often tapping into cutting-edge technology. To stay current and take advantage of innovation, you must explore and embrace these updates.

6. Personalization: Your iPhone should reflect you. Customizing it to your preferences, from the Lock Screen to your app layout, not only adds a personal touch but also enhances usability.

7. Confidence: Understanding your iPhone fosters confidence in using it. No more frustration or feeling overwhelmed. You'll be in control, maximizing its potential effortlessly.

8. Fun: Beyond its practical uses, your iPhone offers entertainment and leisure. From gaming to streaming, photography to music, there's a world of fun waiting for you to discover.

9. Efficiency: In today's fast-paced world, time is precious. Your iPhone can streamline tasks, from managing your schedule to helping you find information instantly. The more you know about its capabilities, the more efficiently you can navigate your daily life.

10. Security: Knowledge is your best defense. Learning how to use security features ensures your data and personal information remain safe.

11. Adaptability: Your iPhone is a tool that adapts to your needs. Learning how to use its features allows it to evolve alongside you, enhancing its value over time.

In essence, getting the most out of your iPhone is not just about technology; it's about empowering yourself to live a more connected, efficient, and enjoyable life. This guide is your key to unlocking this potential, starting with iOS 17.0.1, the latest and greatest version of the iPhone's operating system. So, let's dive in and transform your iPhone into a true companion for every aspect of your life.

1.3 What are the benefits of using all of the features in iOS 17.0.1?

iOS 17.0.1 is more than just a software update; it's a gateway to an enhanced iPhone experience. Here, we unveil the myriad advantages that come with fully embracing the features of iOS 17.0.

1. Customizable Lock Screen:

- Aesthetic Appeal: iOS 17.0.1 empowers you to transform your Lock Screen into a personalized masterpiece. Customize it with widgets, fonts, and wallpapers that resonate with your style, making your iPhone truly your own.

- Functionality: Beyond aesthetics, your Lock Screen becomes a functional hub with widgets that provide at-a-glance information, ensuring your device serves you more efficiently.

2. Focus Mode Enhancements:

- Productivity Boost: Focus mode, now with new features like Focus filters and Focus schedules, empowers you to reclaim your productivity. Hide distractions, stay concentrated on tasks, and automate mode switching based on your location or schedule.

- Mental Well-being: Focus mode also contributes to your well-being by helping you strike a balance between digital engagement and personal time, reducing stress and promoting mental health.

3. Messages App Improvements:

- Effortless Communication: iOS 17.0.1 elevates your communication game. Edit and unsend messages for more precise conversations, mark messages as unread to revisit them later, and collaborate on documents in real time, simplifying your connections with friends and family.

4. Unveiling New Features:

- Live Text for Videos: Unlock a new dimension of interaction with videos by selecting and interacting with text within them, enhancing your understanding and engagement.

- Shared Photo Library: Simplify photo sharing among friends and family by creating a shared library, promoting seamless collaboration.

- Accessibility Advancements: iOS 17.0.1 introduces new accessibility features, ensuring that your iPhone caters to a wider range of users, promoting inclusivity.

5. Overall Empowerment:

- Powerful Efficiency: iOS 17.0.1 optimizes your iPhone's functionality, allowing you to do more with less effort, thereby increasing your overall efficiency.

- Enhanced User Experience: By embracing the full spectrum of features, you'll discover new dimensions of user experience that make your daily tasks more enjoyable.

6. Future-Proofing:

- Stay Current: Keeping up with iOS updates ensures you're on the cutting edge of technology, ready to adapt to future advancements seamlessly.

- Security: Many updates include security enhancements, safeguarding your data and privacy.

7. Enriched Personalization:

- Tailored to You: By utilizing features, you can tailor your iPhone to your preferences, making it an extension of your personality.

8. Connectivity and Engagement:

- Stay Connected: iOS 17.0.1 fosters better connectivity, making it easier to communicate and engage with friends, family, and colleagues.

9. Lifelong Learning:

- Expand Your Knowledge: Exploring new features is an opportunity to learn and grow, enriching your digital literacy.

In essence, using all the features in iOS 17.0.1 transforms your iPhone into a multifaceted tool that not only simplifies your daily life but also enhances your productivity, well-being, and overall user experience. It's the key to unlocking the full potential of your device, making it a seamless extension of your lifestyle.

In the next chapter, we'll take a closer look at the new Lock Screen customization options in iOS 17.0.1. We'll show you how to add widgets, change the font, and choose a wallpaper that you love.

Chapter 2: Lock Screen customization

2.1 How to customize your Lock Screen with widgets, fonts, and wallpapers

The redesigned Lock Screen in iOS 17.0.1 is one of the most significant changes to the iPhone, and it gives you more control over how your Lock Screen looks and functions. With a few simple taps, you can add widgets, change the font, and choose a wallpaper that you love.

1. To customize your Lock Screen, press and hold on an empty area of the screen until you see the Customize button. Tap Customize to open the Lock Screen gallery.

2. Here, you can choose from a variety of pre-made Lock Screens, or you can create your own custom Lock Screen. To create a custom Lock Screen, tap the + button in the top-right corner of the screen.

3. Once you've chosen a Lock Screen, you can start customizing it. To add widgets, tap the + button above the time. You can add up to two widgets to the top of your Lock Screen, and up to four widgets to the bottom.

4. To change the font of the time and date, tap the Clock widget. Then, tap the Font option and choose the font that you like best.

5. To change your wallpaper, tap the Wallpaper & Lock Screen button at the bottom of the screen. Then, choose a wallpaper from your library, or download a new wallpaper from the App Store.

Once you're finished customizing your Lock Screen, tap Done to save your changes.

2.2 How to add multiple widgets to your Lock Screen

Adding multiple widgets to your Lock Screen is a fantastic way to access important information at a glance. Here's a step-by-step guide to get you started:

1. Access Customization: Begin by pressing and holding on an empty area of your Lock Screen. This action will trigger the customization mode.

2. Enter the Lock Screen Gallery: Once you've activated customization, tap the "Customize" button that appears. This action opens up the Lock Screen gallery, where you can make your desired changes.

3. Initiate Widget Addition: To add widgets, focus on the area above the current time display on your Lock Screen. You'll notice a '+' button; tap it.

4. Select Widgets: Upon tapping the '+' button, a list of available widgets will appear. Choose the widgets you want to add to your Lock Screen. You can select multiple widgets to display.

5. Repeat as Needed: If you'd like to add more widgets, simply tap the '+' button again and choose additional widgets. You can repeat this step until you've added all the widgets you desire.

6. Save Your Changes: Once you've customized your Lock Screen with the desired widgets, tap the "Done" button to save your changes. Your Lock Screen now boasts a wealth of information and functionality.

By following these steps, you can transform your Lock Screen into a dynamic and informative dashboard, giving you quick access to the data that matters most to you. Whether it's weather updates, calendar events, or news headlines, your Lock Screen can now be a powerful tool for staying informed.

2.3 How to change the font of the time and date

If you're someone who appreciates the finer details of personalization, changing the font of the time and date on your Lock Screen can be a delightful touch. Here's a step-by-step guide to help you achieve this:

1. Initiate Customization: Start by pressing and holding an empty area on your Lock Screen. This action will trigger the customization mode, unlocking your ability to make personalized changes.

2. Access the Lock Screen Gallery: Upon activating customization, look for and tap the "Customize" button that appears. This opens the Lock Screen gallery, where you can make various adjustments.

3. Focus on the Clock Widget: Inside the Lock Screen gallery, you'll see various elements that you can customize. Locate and tap on the "Clock" widget.

4. Font Selection: By tapping the Clock widget, you'll reveal a range of options. Among these options is "Font." Tap on it to explore the available font choices.

5. Choose Your Preferred Font: Browse through the fonts presented to you and select the one that resonates with your style and preference. The font you choose will be applied to the time and date display on your Lock Screen.

6. Save Your Font Selection: After making your font choice, tap "Done" to save your changes. Your Lock Screen will now showcase the time and date in your selected font.

With these straightforward steps, you can add a touch of personal flair to your Lock Screen. It's a small adjustment that can make a significant difference in how your iPhone reflects your individuality. Enjoy the new look of your Lock Screen with your chosen font!

In the next chapter, we'll take a look at the Focus mode improvements in iOS 17.0.1. We'll show you how to create different Focus modes for different activities, and how to use Focus filters and schedules to get the most out of Focus mode.

Chapter 3: Focus mode

3.1 What is Focus mode?

Focus mode is a dynamic and productivity-boosting feature integrated into iOS, designed to help you stay on track and minimize distractions in our fast-paced digital world. It's your personal assistant for managing your attention and ensuring that your iPhone works in harmony with your tasks and activities.

Key Aspects of Focus Mode:

1. Enhanced Productivity: At its core, Focus mode is a tool to enhance your productivity. It understands that there are specific times when you need to focus on work, study, or even just relax. By enabling Focus mode, you're signaling to your iPhone that it should adapt to your current needs.

2. Distraction Reduction: One of the primary functions of Focus mode is to reduce distractions. It does this by allowing you to select which apps and notifications are permitted to interrupt you while you're in a Focus mode. This way, you can concentrate without the constant barrage of notifications.

3. Personalization: Focus mode is highly customizable. You can create different Focus modes for various activities, tailoring each one to your specific requirements. For instance, you can have a "Work" Focus mode that only allows work-related apps and notifications, and a "Study" Focus mode for your study sessions.

4. Automation: With Focus mode, you can automate the process of enabling and disabling it. This is where it becomes even more powerful. You can set up schedules that activate certain Focus modes based on your location or the time of day. For instance, your "Work" Focus mode can automatically activate when you reach your workplace.

5. Peace of Mind: Beyond enhancing productivity, Focus mode contributes to your well-being. It allows you to strike a balance between your digital life and personal time. By muting non-essential notifications during your relaxation periods, you gain peace of mind.

In essence, Focus mode empowers you to take control of your iPhone, ensuring it aligns with your goals and activities. It's a feature that embraces the idea that technology should serve you, not distract you. With Focus mode, you can unlock your iPhone's potential to help you achieve your tasks efficiently and enjoy moments of undistracted focus.

3.2 How to create different Focus modes for different activities

Creating different Focus modes tailored to various activities is a fantastic way to optimize your iPhone for different parts of your day. Whether it's work, studying, or leisure, Focus mode has you covered. Here's how to set up these personalized modes step by step:

Step 1: Access Your Settings

- Begin by unlocking your iPhone and navigating to the home screen. From there, locate and tap the "Settings" app, which usually appears as a gear icon.

Step 2: Enter the Focus Section

- Scroll through the list of options in the Settings app until you find "Focus." It's typically located near the top of the menu, but you can use the search bar at the top of the screen to quickly locate it if needed.

Step 3: Create a New Focus Mode

- Inside the "Focus" section, you'll find various pre-existing Focus modes. To create a new one, look for a '+' button in the top-right corner of the screen. Tap it to initiate the process.

Step 4: Name Your Focus Mode

- Now, you have the opportunity to give your new Focus mode a name. This name should reflect the purpose of the mode, making it easy to identify later. For instance, you might name it "Work" or "Study."

Step 5: Select Allowed Apps and Notifications

- After naming your Focus mode, tap "Choose" to start selecting which apps and notifications are allowed when this Focus mode is active. You can customize this list to suit your specific needs for this particular activity.

Step 6: Save Your Focus Mode

- Once you've configured your new Focus mode by selecting the allowed apps and notifications, tap "Done" to save your settings.

Step 7: Repeat for Additional Modes

- If you want to create more Focus modes for different activities, simply repeat these steps. You can create as many as you need to cover your work, study, relaxation, or any other scenarios.

With these personalized Focus modes, your iPhone becomes a versatile tool that adapts to your day's demands. It ensures that you receive the right notifications and have access to the appropriate apps depending on your current activity. By following these steps, you can take full advantage of Focus mode's customization capabilities and stay focused and productive throughout your day.

3.3 How to use Focus filters to hide certain apps and notifications from specific Focus modes

Focus filters are your secret weapon for fine-tuning your Focus modes and reducing distractions to a minimum. They allow you to hide specific apps and notifications from particular Focus modes, ensuring your iPhone adapts precisely to your needs. Here's a step-by-step guide on how to use Focus filters:

Step 1: Access Your Settings

- Start by unlocking your iPhone and locating the "Settings" app on your home screen. It typically appears as a gear icon.

Step 2: Enter the Focus Section

- Scroll through the list of settings options until you find "Focus." Tap on it to enter the Focus settings.

Step 3: Choose a Focus Mode

- Within the Focus settings, you'll see a list of your existing Focus modes. Choose the one to which you want to add a filter by tapping on it.

Step 4: Add a Filter

- Inside your selected Focus mode settings, scroll down until you find the "Add Filter" option. Tap on it to begin the process.

Step 5: Select Filter Type

- Focus modes offer two types of filters: App and People. Choose the filter type that aligns with your goals. For instance, you can select "App" to hide notifications from specific apps during this Focus mode.

Step 6: Configure Your Filter

- Once you've selected the filter type, you'll need to configure it according to your preferences. If you're creating an app filter, you'll see a list of apps installed on your device. Simply select the apps you want to hide during this Focus mode.

Step 7: Save the Filter

- After you've fine-tuned your filter settings, tap "Done" to save your filter. This filter will now be active during the selected Focus mode.

Step 8: Repeat as Needed

- If you want to add more filters to the same Focus mode or create filters for different Focus modes, simply repeat these steps.

Focus filters are highly versatile and allow you to tailor your Focus modes to the specifics of your activities. For instance, you can hide social media apps when using your "Work" Focus mode to boost productivity. By following these straightforward steps, you can fine-tune your Focus modes to eliminate the distractions that hinder your focus and productivity, allowing you to stay on track with your tasks.

3.4 How to use Focus schedules to automatically enable and disable Focus modes based on your location or time of day

Focus schedules are a brilliant way to automate the activation and deactivation of your Focus modes, ensuring that your iPhone aligns with your daily routine effortlessly. You can set them to activate based on your location or specific times of the day. Here's a step-by-step guide on how to use Focus schedules:

Step 1: Access Your Settings

- Begin by unlocking your iPhone and locating the "Settings" app on your home screen. It's typically represented by a gear icon.

Step 2: Enter the Focus Section

- Scroll through the list of settings until you find "Focus." Tap on it to access the Focus settings.

Step 3: Select a Focus Mode

- Inside the Focus settings, choose the Focus mode to which you want to add a schedule by tapping on it.

Step 4: Add a Schedule

- Within your selected Focus mode settings, scroll down until you see the "Add Schedule" option. Tap on it to initiate the scheduling process.

Step 5: Choose Schedule Type

- Focus modes offer two scheduling options: location-based and time-based. Select the type that suits your needs. For instance, you can opt for a time-based schedule to activate your "Work" Focus mode every weekday from 9 AM to 5 PM.

Step 6: Configure Your Schedule

- Depending on your chosen schedule type, configure the settings accordingly. If it's a time-based schedule, specify the start and end times. If it's location-based, select your desired location.

Step 7: Save the Schedule

- After you've set up your schedule preferences, tap "Done" to save the schedule. Your Focus mode will now automatically activate and deactivate according to the schedule you've defined.

Step 8: Repeat as Needed

- If you want to create schedules for other Focus modes or additional schedules for the same mode, simply repeat these steps.

With Focus schedules, you can seamlessly transition between different Focus modes without the need for manual adjustments. For example, you can have your "Work" Focus mode activate automatically when you arrive at your workplace or deactivate it when you leave.

Alternatively, you can ensure that your "Sleep" Focus mode kicks in at your bedtime without any manual intervention.

By following these straightforward steps, you can take full advantage of Focus schedules to enhance your productivity and maintain your focus without the hassle of manual mode adjustments. It's an effective way to ensure that your iPhone adapts to your daily routine effortlessly.

In the next chapter, we'll take a look at the Messages improvements in iOS 17.0.1. We'll show you how to edit and unsend messages, mark messages as unread, and collaborate on documents in real time.

Chapter 4: Messages improvements

4.1 How to edit and unsend messages

In iOS 17.0.1, the Messages app introduces a game-changing feature: the ability to edit and unsend messages. This means that the occasional typos, auto-correct mishaps, or regrettable messages can now be rectified or retracted with ease. Here's how to make the most of this feature:

Step 1: Access the Messages App

Begin by unlocking your iPhone and locating the Messages app. It's the one with the speech bubble icon, usually found on your home screen.

Step 2: Locate the Message

Scroll through your list of conversations to find the message you want to edit or unsend.

Step 3: Tap and Hold

To initiate the message editing or unsending options, tap and hold your finger on the message in question. This action will bring up a menu.

Step 4: Choose Edit or Undo Send

From the menu that appears, you have two options: "**Edit**" and "**Undo Send**." Select "**Edit**" if you want to make changes to the message, or choose "Undo Send" if you wish to completely retract the message.

Step 5: Make Your Edits

If you selected "**Edit**," you can now modify the message. Correct typos, clarify your message, or amend it as necessary. Once your edits are complete, tap "**Done**" to save the changes.

Note: You have a window of up to 15 minutes after sending a message to either edit or unsend it. Keep in mind that if the recipient has already read the message, they might still see the original content before your edit or unsending takes effect.

This invaluable feature ensures that your messaging is more accurate, and it gives you the power to quickly correct any communication mishaps. iOS 17.0.1's message editing and unsending capabilities provide a level of control and convenience that makes your messaging experience smoother than ever.

You can edit or unsend a message for up to 15 minutes after you've sent it. However, keep in mind that if the recipient has already read the message, they may still be able to see the original message before you edit or unsend it.

4.2 How to mark messages as unread

iOS 17.0.1 introduces a handy feature in the Messages app that allows you to mark messages as unread. This feature is particularly useful when you're busy and need a reminder to respond to a message at a more convenient time. Here's how to use it:

Step 1: Open the Messages App

Begin by unlocking your iPhone and locating the Messages app. It's the one with the speech bubble icon, typically found on your home screen.

Step 2: Locate the Message

Within the Messages app, scroll through your list of conversations to find the message you want to mark as unread.

Step 3: Swipe Left and Tap Mark as Unread

To mark a message as unread, swipe left on the message you wish to mark. This action will reveal a menu. From the menu, tap "Mark as Unread."

Once you've marked a message as unread, it will appear at the top of your message list and be visually distinct to remind you to respond or revisit it later.

This feature offers a practical way to manage your messages, ensuring you never overlook an important message that requires your attention. Whether you're in a rush or simply need a reminder, marking messages as unread in iOS 17.0.1 makes it easy to stay on top of your conversations.

4.3 How to collaborate on documents in real time

iOS 17.0.1 enhances your messaging experience with a powerful feature: real-time document collaboration within the Messages app. This is an excellent way to work on projects, share ideas, or make edits together with friends, family, or colleagues. Here's how to make the most of this collaborative feature:

Step 1: Access the Messages App

Start by unlocking your iPhone and locating the Messages app. It's the app with a speech bubble icon, usually found on your home screen.

Step 2: Begin a Conversation

Initiate a conversation with the individuals you want to collaborate with. This can be a group chat or a one-on-one conversation, depending on your needs.

Step 3: Share a Document

Within the conversation, tap the '+' button located in the bottom-left corner of the screen. This action will bring up a menu of options.

From the menu, select "**Share**" and then choose "**Document**."

Step 4: Pick the Document

Next, select the document you want to collaborate on. You can choose a document from your files, cloud storage, or any other accessible location.

Step 5: Initiate Collaboration

Once you've selected the document, tap "**Collaborate**."

A link to the document will be sent to all participants in the conversation. They can click on the link to access the document and start collaborating in real time.

During the collaboration, you can see the changes that others are making to the document as they happen. This real-time collaboration is complemented by the ability to chat with others in the same conversation about the document, making it a seamless and efficient way to work together, regardless of your physical location.

This feature is especially valuable for teams, students, or anyone who needs to collaborate on documents quickly and effortlessly. Whether you're making edits, brainstorming ideas, or working on a project, real-time document collaboration in iOS 17.0.1's Messages app makes teamwork more accessible and efficient than ever before.

In the next chapter, we'll take a look at some of the other new features in iOS 17.0.1, such as Live Text for videos, Shared Photo Library, and new accessibility features.

Chapter 5: Other new features

In addition to the new features that we've already covered in this book, iOS 17.0.1 also includes a number of other new features, such as Live Text for videos, Shared Photo Library, and new accessibility features.

5.1 Live Text for videos

Live Text, a feature first introduced for images in iOS, has been expanded in iOS 17.0.1 to include videos. This innovative feature allows you to interact with text within paused video frames, offering a range of possibilities. Here's a step-by-step guide on how to use Live Text for videos:

Step 1: Access a Video

Open any video, whether it's in your Photos app, Camera app, or any other video-compatible application.

Step 2: Pause the Video

Pause the video at the frame where you want to interact with the text.

Step 3: Tap and Hold

To select and interact with text within the video frame, tap and hold your finger on the desired text.

Step 4: Select Text

A selection box will appear around the text you tapped. Now, you have various options, including copying, pasting, translating, or looking up the selected text.

Live Text for videos offers a wide range of practical applications. For instance, you can use it to translate subtitles in foreign-language videos, extract information from educational videos, or simply engage more deeply with video content. This feature enhances your video-watching experience by making the text within videos accessible and actionable, giving you more control and utility over your multimedia interactions.

5.2 Shared Photo Library

iOS 17.0.1 introduces a convenient and collaborative way to manage and share your photos through the Shared Photo Library feature. Instead of manually sending individual photos to friends and family, you can create a Shared Photo Library that up to five people can access and contribute to. Here's a step-by-step guide on how to use this feature:

Step 1: Open the Photos App

Begin by unlocking your iPhone and opening the Photos app. This app is represented by a multi-colored flower icon and is commonly found on your home screen.

Step 2: Start a Shared Photo Library

Inside the Photos app, tap the '+' button located in the top-left corner of the screen. This action will initiate the process of creating a Shared Photo Library.

Step 3: Create a Shared Photo Library

Select "Shared Photo Library" from the available options. This choice will enable you to create a new Shared Photo Library.

Step 4: Name Your Library

Give your Shared Photo Library a unique name. This name helps you and your collaborators identify the library easily.

Step 5: Invite Collaborators

After creating the Shared Photo Library, you can invite up to five people to join. They will receive an invitation to become collaborators.

Step 6: Collaborate on Photos and Videos

Once the Shared Photo Library is established and collaborators are added, all participants can collectively manage the photos and videos within the library. This includes adding, editing, and deleting content. Additionally, you can easily share new photos and videos directly to the Shared Photo Library from various apps on your device.

Shared Photo Library simplifies photo sharing, keeps all shared photos neatly organized in one place, and promotes seamless collaboration on albums with friends and family. It's a user-friendly feature designed to enhance the way you manage and share your cherished memories.

5.3 New Accessibility Features

iOS 17.0.1 introduces several new accessibility features, designed to make the iPhone even more inclusive and user-friendly. These features cater to a diverse range of needs and enhance the overall accessibility of the device. Here's a closer look at each of these new accessibility features:

Door Detection:

Door Detection is a groundbreaking addition that utilizes the LiDAR scanner available on iPhone 12 Pro and later models. It aims to assist individuals who are blind or have low vision by detecting doors and providing relevant information about them. This information includes whether the door is open or closed and whether it has a handle. Door Detection enhances spatial awareness and helps users navigate their surroundings with greater confidence.

Live Captions:

Live Captions is a real-time captioning feature designed to benefit individuals who are deaf or hard of hearing. It provides captions for any audio or video content on your iPhone. This feature ensures that users can follow and understand content, even in noisy environments or when sound is unavailable. Live Captions improve accessibility across various apps and media content, making the iPhone more inclusive for all users.

VoiceOver Enhancements:

VoiceOver is a built-in screen reader that reads aloud everything displayed on the screen, making iOS accessible to individuals with visual impairments. In iOS 17.0.1, VoiceOver receives significant enhancements:

- Gesture Controls: Users can now control VoiceOver using gestures, offering a more intuitive and responsive experience. This enhances navigation and interaction for VoiceOver users.
- Pitch and Speed Adjustment: iOS 17.0.1 introduces the ability to adjust the pitch and speed of VoiceOver's speech output. This customization allows users to fine-tune the VoiceOver experience to suit their preferences.

These accessibility features represent Apple's commitment to ensuring that the iPhone is accessible to all users, regardless of their abilities. By continually expanding and improving accessibility options, iOS 17.0.1 enhances the usability and inclusivity of the iPhone, making it a versatile and accommodating device for individuals with diverse needs.

In the next chapter, we'll take a look at some tips and tricks for getting the most out of iOS 17.0.1. We'll show you how to use Spotlight to search for anything, use Siri to get things done, use gestures to navigate your iPhone, and use iCloud to keep your data backed up.

Chapter 6: Tips and tricks

In this chapter, we'll take a look at some tips and tricks for getting the most out of iOS 17.0.1.

6.1 How to use Spotlight to search for anything

Spotlight is a versatile search tool in iOS 17.0.1 that allows you to find virtually anything on your iPhone with ease. Here's how to harness its power:

1. Access Spotlight: You can open Spotlight from anywhere on your iPhone's Home Screen by swiping down from the middle of the screen. It's a quick and convenient way to initiate your search.

2. Start Typing: As soon as Spotlight is active, you can start typing your search query. The search begins instantly, scouring your iPhone for various types of

content, including apps, contacts, messages, files, and more.

3. Suggested Results: Spotlight is not just a search bar; it's a smart tool that provides real-time suggestions as you type. These suggestions help you refine your search. You can tap on any of these suggestions to open the relevant result, or continue typing to narrow down your search further.

Spotlight is a powerful tool for finding anything on your iPhone swiftly. It's not only an efficient way to locate specific items but also a great way to stumble upon new features and apps you might not have explored yet.

6.2 How to use Siri to get things done

Siri, Apple's voice assistant, is your handy companion for executing tasks on your iPhone with just your voice.

Here's a comprehensive guide on how to make the most of Siri:

1. Activation: Siri can be activated in two ways:
   - "Hey Siri": If you've enabled this feature in your settings, simply say "Hey Siri," and Siri will spring to life, ready to assist.
   - Side Button (or Home Button): Alternatively, you can press and hold the Side button (or the Home button on older devices) to activate Siri.

2. Voice Commands: Once Siri is listening, you can issue various voice commands to accomplish a wide array of tasks:
   - Communication: Make phone calls, send text messages, or even compose and send emails hands-free.

   - Alarms and Reminders: Set alarms, timers, and reminders effortlessly.
   - Information: Ask Siri for directions, weather forecasts, sports scores, and general knowledge questions.

- Media: Play music, podcasts, audiobooks, and even control playback with voice commands.

- App Launching: Open apps and websites by simply instructing Siri.

- Smart Home Control: Manage smart home devices, such as lights, thermostats, and more, using your voice.

3. Stay Connected: Siri isn't just a taskmaster; it's a conversational assistant that keeps you connected and informed. You can engage Siri in natural language conversations and ask follow-up questions to dive deeper into tasks or gather more information.

Siri is your key to hands-free productivity and convenience on your iPhone. Whether you're on the move, multitasking, or simply want to simplify your interactions with your device, Siri is your trusty companion for getting things done.

6.3 How to use gestures to navigate your iPhone

iOS includes a variety of intuitive gestures that make navigating your iPhone a breeze. Here's a guide to some of the most common and useful gestures:

1. Swipe Left or Right: You can swiftly switch between open apps by swiping left or right on the screen. This gesture lets you move seamlessly between your recently used apps, making multitasking effortless.

2. Swipe Up from the Bottom: Swiping up from the bottom of the screen opens the Control Center. Here, you can access essential settings like Wi-Fi, Bluetooth, screen brightness, and more. It's a quick way to adjust settings without leaving your current app.

3. Swipe Down from the Top-Right Corner: This action opens the Notification Center, displaying your notifications and widgets. It's a convenient way to stay updated on messages, emails, and calendar events.

4. Tap and Hold on the Home Screen: To enter Jiggle mode, tap and hold on the Home Screen. In this mode, you can rearrange app icons, create app folders, and delete apps by tapping the "X" that appears in the corner of app icons.

5. Pinch to Zoom: You can use a pinch gesture (spreading two fingers apart or bringing them together) to zoom in and out on content like photos, maps, and webpages.

These gestures are designed to streamline your iPhone experience, allowing you to navigate and interact with your device more efficiently. Experiment with them to discover which gestures work best for you and your daily tasks.

6.4 How to use iCloud to keep your data backed up

iCloud is Apple's cloud storage service, and it can be used to keep your data backed up and accessible from all of your devices. To enable iCloud backup, go to Settings > [Your Name] > iCloud > iCloud Backup.

Once iCloud backup is enabled, iCloud will automatically back up your iPhone's data on a regular basis. This includes your photos, videos, contacts, messages, and more.

If you lose your iPhone or if it's damaged, you can restore your data from iCloud. To do this, simply sign in to iCloud on your new iPhone and choose to restore from a backup.

iCloud is a great way to keep your data safe and accessible. It's also a great way to easily transfer data between your iPhone and other devices.

In the next chapter, we'll conclude our guide to iOS 17.0.1 by recapping the key takeaways and providing resources for learning more.

Chapter 7: Conclusion

In this book, we've learned all about the new features and improvements in iOS 17.0.1. We've also learned some tips and tricks for getting the most out of your iPhone.

Here is a recap of the key takeaways from this book:

1. iOS 17.0.1 includes a number of new features, such as a redesigned Lock Screen, Focus mode improvements, Messages improvements, and other new features such as Live Text for videos, Shared Photo Library, and new accessibility features.

2. To get the most out of iOS 17.0.1, you should customize your Lock Screen, use Focus mode to stay focused and reduce distractions, check out the new Messages features, and explore the other new features.

3. Some tips and tricks for getting the most out of iOS 17.0.1 include using Spotlight to search for anything, using Siri to get things done, using gestures to navigate your iPhone, and using iCloud to keep your data backed up.

Resources for learning more about iOS 17.0.1

If you want to learn more about iOS 17.0.1, here are a few resources:

- The official Apple website: https://www.apple.com/ios/ios-17/
- The Apple support website: https://support.apple.com/ios
- YouTube channels such as WWDC and Apple
- Tech websites such as The Verge, Ars Technica, and Engadget

We hope you enjoyed this guide to iOS 17.0.1. If you have any questions or feedback, please let us know in the through a review

What is one thing that you learned from this chapter that you're excited to try on your iPhone?